The Edie and Elmira Show

PAUL D. PATTON

Integratio Press
Pasco, Washington

THE EDIE AND ELMIRA SHOW

Trinity House is a Division of Integratio Press
Integratio Press is the Imprint of the Christianity and Communication
Studies Network
11503 Easton Dr.
Pasco, WA 99301

www.theccsn.com

Cover design: Katie Dennison
Interior design: Mary Bryant
Image: Wikimedia Commons Internet Archive Book Images, and Adobe Stock

paperback isbn: 978-1-959685-05-0
ebook isbn: 978-1-959685-06-7

Library of Congress Control Number: 2023945327

About the Author

PAUL PATTON (PhD, Regent University) is Professor Emeritus of Communication and Theater at Spring Arbor University in Michigan. It was while pastoring at Trinity Church in Livonia, Michigan, that he founded Trinity House Theater in 1981. He is the author of over 30 produced stage plays, radio plays, and performance essays. He is contributing author to the books, *Understanding Evangelical Media* (IVP), *Evangelical Christians and Popular Culture* (Praeger), and *Prophetic Critique and Popular Culture* (Peter Lang), and co-author of *Prophetically (In)Correct: A Christian Introduction to Media Criticism* (Brazos Press), and the newly published, *Everyday Sabbath: How to Lead Your Dance with Media and Technology in Mindful and Sacred Ways* (Cascade Books).

Author's Note

I BECAME INTERESTED first in the Andersonville prison camp's history of atrocities committed against Union soldiers in the Confederate state of Georgia but changed my focus to the atrocities inflicted on Confederate soldiers in the Union prison in Elmira, New York. What deepened my interest in the horrors of the Northern prison camp was reading about the observation towers built adjacent to the prison walls by entrepreneurs and the paralleling secret tunnels underneath the walls, where three Confederate prisoners would escape in 1864. The owner of the tower charged Northern citizens 15 cents to climb the towers and gawk at the prisoners below. Refreshments were sold. Then another tower was built by a separate owner, and, competition for customers being what it is/was, the entrance fee was reduced to 10 cents.

My interest in the shock-television styles of Jerry Springer, Phil Donahue, and others in the 1980s and 90s grew into my own daily "fix" on the appallingly inhumane confessions of guests on the show. I became, along with a good percentage of Americans, ready and willing to witness the degradations and near-damning testimonials of guests drenched in the possibility of having their lurid tales rise above the impotence of anonymity.

In 1989, editorialist and television news commentator Charles Krauthammer quipped,

> In the age of (Phil) Donahue, the commandment is "Love thyself, then thy neighbor." The formulation is a license for unremitting self-indulgence, since the quest for self-love is never finished and since the obligation to love others must be deferred while the search continues. No distractions please, first things first.

> -Charles Kraughthammer, *The Detroit News*, May 9, 1989.

Historical Note

ELMIRA PRISON OPENED in July of 1864 and closed the following July. The Southern prisoners commonly referred to the prison as "Hellmira," with almost 3,000 of the 12,100 prisoners dying from a combination of malnutrition, exposure to winter temperatures (many prisoners without coats and seeing snow for the first time), and diseases spread by poor sanitary conditions.

Very quickly, with the construction of two observation towers charging Northern citizens to climb and gawk at the rebel soldiers below, the outside acreage surrounding the camp took on a very festive atmosphere. Refreshments were sold to the onlookers. And just as quickly, the prisoners came to resent the pointing and gawking from the towers and began to mockingly pantomime circus-animal antics. As winter approached, the towers lost most of their customers, the prisoners were left without an audience, and many of them froze without winter attire.

That winter (1864-65) was especially cold, with temperatures dipping twice to -18. That February, a snowstorm dropped over two feet of snow.

The prisoners built tunnels under the prison walls to escape to the Southern states. There were many attempts, but in the end, only ten prisoners were successful.

The mortality rate at the Elmira prison (24.5%) nearly matched the mortality rate of the South's Andersonville prison (28.7%).

Production Note

THE EDIE AND ELMIRA SHOW premiered in the late 1990s at Regent University and subsequently played at Spring Arbor University in 2009.

In the Spring Arbor production, performed in an auditorium with 350 seats and a traditionally sized staging area, Elmira Prison scenes took place stage left and the Edie McDonald show was on stage right. This made for quick and efficient transitions. For the Edie McDonald scenes, television cameras projected image close-ups of Edie and her guests on a large screen, pushing audiences to decide whether to witness the live action or the enlarged screen images.

Cast of Characters

(in order of appearance)

Lionel Stubbs	Confederate prisoner
Elton Crimmons	Confederate prisoner and friend of Lionel
Stagehands	
Caleb Smith	Confederate prisoner, mute
Edie McDonald	Television talk show host, dynamic, always ready to entertain.
A few audience members	Shouting their love for Edie McDonald
Anna Johnson	First guest on Edie's show
Steve Morgan	Second guest
Director/Producer of show	
Camera operator	
Onlookers	
Bill McDonald	Edie's husband
Uniformed security officer	

Scene One

SETTING: Rope is attached to the top of four wooden poles standing at each STAGE corner. A SIGN reading "Elmira Federal Prison" is hung on one DOWNSTAGE pole. The following historical note is PROJECTED onto a SCREEN:

> **In the summer of 1864, an entrepreneur built an observation tower just outside the walls of the federal prison at Elmira, New York. He charged 15 cents for citizens to climb the tower and observe the Confederate prisoners below. Ginger cakes and drinks were sold. The venture paid for itself in a matter of weeks. Shortly afterward another observation tower was constructed by another business interest and, competition being what it is, the cost for admission was driven to ten cents. Business was booming. Then the winter came.**

AT RISE: With the house dark, a Stephen FOSTER melody fills the theater with an overarching, mood-setting presence. After a few moments, a successive layer of audio snippets crescendo—canned laughter, broken sentences of Edie McDonald show, riffs of Jimi Hendrix's cover of Bob Dylan's "All Along the Watchtower," sounds of precision troops marching—swelling into a loud cacophony of disorienting noise. Each layer is then successively removed, ending with the Foster melody.

(After a few moments, OFFSTAGE, a HARMONICA is played poorly, perhaps the faintly recognizable "DIXIE.")

(LIONEL STUBBS walks ONSTAGE playing the harmonica. HE is wearing the worn, tattered uniform of the Confederate soldier.)

(A SHOUT from OFFSTAGE—)

OFFSTAGE VOICE

Stop with that sorry music!!

LIONEL

What music you talking about? That Foster creation I hear every morning 'bout this time, or my humble attempt to entertain my bored self?

(ELTON CRIMMONS enters, wearing similar Confederate garb.)

ELTON

What Foster music, you ol' fool? You're the only one hearin' any Stephen Foster music! What you keep talkin' 'bout Foster music you hearin'? I'm talking 'bout you and your sorry, too stinkin' to be sanctified, har-mon-i-ca playin', those sounds that would kill a high-flyin' crow and make a grown man weep in the misery of it all.

(The FOSTER MUSIC stops.)

LIONEL

There the music stopped.

ELTON

I ain't hearin' no music, Lionel. I'd like to hear some music, somethin' other than your harmonica.

LIONEL

How, Mr. Elton T. Crimmons, am I goin' ta get any better unless I keep playin'?

(LIONEL starts to play.)

ELTON

Lord have mercy!

> (HE LAUGHS, playfully tries to grab at harmonica)

Blessed are the merciful, Lionel, for they shall obtain mercy!

> (LIONEL keeps playing, enjoying the exchange. HE playfully keeps the harmonica just out of arms reach. ELTON gets LIONEL in a modified headlock.)

LIONEL

Then be merciful, son!

ELTON

Give me the harmonica, ol' man!

> (LIONEL tucks HIS head lower, buries the harmonica in HIS clenched fists, after managing to get off a last few pathetic notes.)
>
> (LOUD BANGING, hammers to nails is heard in the back of the theatre.)
>
> (ELTON and LIONEL abruptly disengage, raise THEIR heads in query—)

ELTON (cont.)

And what in heaven's lovely name was that?

> (LIONEL mischievously blows another measure into the harmonica. LAUGHS.)

LIONEL

Nothin' but another Yankee handcraft project. We whittles pipes and walkin' sticks and other meanin'ful knick-knacks, and they makes another fortification. Eltie, it ain't nothin' but another Yankee handcraft project.

> (Two STAGEHANDS carry on the first section of the platform to the back of the theatre. . . .)

ELTON

Well, lookie there. What you think it is?

> (ELTON moves closer to the edge of the STAGE, the imaginary prison fence. . . .)

LIONEL

You watch yourself gettin' too close to that—

> (ELTON is too close. SOUND: A WARNING SHOT is fired. ELTON jumps back.)

LIONEL (cont.)

. . . fence. Eltie, you gotta learn how to approach that there fence with more theatrical flair—

> (HE begins to tiptoe, with overgrown motions, toward the fence. Two feet from the fence, HE stops, slowly moves HIS forefinger closer . . . at about a foot away from the fence, another SHOT is fired.)

LIONEL (cont.)

. . . so them there Feds can activate the twelve inch rule.

> (ELTON joins LIONEL and with drill team accuracy draw THEIR right forefingers toward the fence, and as THEIR fingers get a foot away, another SHOT is fired.)
>
> (ELTON and LIONEL share a big LAUGH.)

ELTON

Do you think them Fed boys aiming for our rebellious pointin' finger?

LIONEL

Them Fed boys aimin' to get home to their New Hampshire coddlin'— that's all them boys aimin' for.

ELTON

You ever think they might one day shoot off your finger?

LIONEL

I'd just have to point things out with the pointin' finger on my
other hand—

> (HE shrivels HIS right hand, points with the forefinger of
> HIS left)

ELTON

As you were givin' the tour.

LIONEL

> (Finds an aristocratic voice)

Ladies and gentle—

ELTON

Don't you call no Yankees gentlemen but do give 'em the grand tour!

LIONEL

Gentlemen, may I point out to you on this fine day the source of all
this summer stench—

> (Clears throat)

the gorgeous, but yellow, —

ELTON

And collector of every kind of filth imagined by the mind—

LIONEL

Foster's Pond, smack in the middle of our fine Elmira Inn—And
if you come back at dusk you can watch the yellow sun sink in the
pond's yellow stench of everyone's pee.

ELTON

How 'bout—

LIONEL/ELTON

a swim!

(THEY both revel in this repeated attempt at humor.)

ELTON

I'll tell you, ol' man, you'd still point things out pretty well, even with your pointing finger blown off.

LIONEL

Thank ya'.

ELTON

You wanna see if we can get 'em to shoot at us again?

LIONEL

Naa, after three shots that heap of humanity Preston yells so robust-like at us vermin privates, and I'm gettin' mighty tired of his Yankee voice—how 'bout you?

(HE starts up with the harmonica.)

(ELTON playfully lunges to grab the harmonica.)

ELTON

Lionel, now stop tryin' to aggravate me!

(LIONEL backpedals, points over the fence as STAGE-HANDS bring on another piece of the platform. STAGE-HANDS will proceed to connect the two pieces during the following exchange. . . .)

LIONEL

Hey, lookie there— somethin' strange goin' on over cross the way.

(THEY look at the STAGEHANDS.)

ELTON

What you think they're doin'?

LIONEL

Sure as shootin' buildin' somethin'.

ELTON

But it sure as shootin' ain't on prison property.

LIONEL

(To STAGEHANDS)

Hey, what you buildin' over there?

(STAGEHANDS keep working.)

LIONEL (cont.)

Hey, you Yankees, what you doin' with all that racket?!

(STAGEHANDS share an unheard joke between themselves and start LAUGHING.)

ELTON

Hey, them folk laughin' at us.

LIONEL

Hey, what's so funny, you Yankees?!

(STAGEHANDS continue to LAUGH between themselves as THEY finish and exit.)

LIONEL (cont.)

I said what you boys laughin' at? You laughin' at us in here?

(Increasing intensity)

Hey, where you goin'?! You laughin' at us?!!

ELTON

Let 'em go, Lionel, ain't worth you all fussin' and—

LIONEL

They laughin' at us, those Yankee bastards are laughin' at us!! I feel like chokin' their cranin' necks. Get me a gun, I'll blow their heads off!!

(LIONEL starts moving closer to fence, accusingly pointing HIS finger at the STAGEHANDS.)

LIONEL (cont.)

I said I'll blow their heads off!!!

> (ELTON attempts to calm LIONEL, tries to block HIM
> from getting closer to the fence.)

ELTON

Lionel, now you calm yourself down! No tellin' what them boys
laughin' at!

> (In the struggle THEY move too close to the fence. Another
> SHOT is fired—LIONEL grabs at HIS hand, SCREAMS,
> writhing in pain. HE falls to the ground, ELTON hovering
> over, tending—then whirling around, looking up to scream
> at the tower from where the shot was fired—)

ELTON (cont.)

Is that you, Preston, you Yankee yellow piss—you just plumb near
shot his hand off!!

> (LIONEL rises, still in great pain, but SHOUTS over the fence—)

LIONEL

> (To STAGEHANDS)

What you laughin' at?!! You laughin' at me?!!

> (The STAGEHANDS enter LAUGHING with the third and
> final piece and commence finishing the platform.)

LIONEL (cont.)

> (SCREAMS)

What you boys laughin' at?!

> (The STAGEHANDS stop, turn to LIONEL and pronounce—)

STAGEHAND

None of your bee's wax what we're laughing at.

> (THEY finish the platform and exit. THEIR LAUGHTER
> now diminished to a CHUCKLE. LIONEL steps back,
> stunned, covering HIS wounded hand.)

ELTON

Let me see that hand, Lionel.

> (LIONEL pulls the hand into HIS body, covers it with HIS other hand, furiously shaking HIS head.)

ELTON (cont.)

Let me see your hand, Lionel!

> (LIONEL hands HIM HIS harmonica as HE continues to shake HIS head, refusing to show HIM HIS wounded hand. LIONEL looks, eyes fixed, at the platform area.)

LIONEL

> (Calmly, trance-like)

What'd he mean, "none of my bee's wax"?

> (ELTON, behind LIONEL, grabs at HIS hand. LIONEL is without energy to resist.)

ELTON

My God, Lionel, they shot off your finger!!

> (SCREAMS up at the tower)

Preston! Get somebody down here to take care of Lionel!!

> (ELTON tears off part of HIS ragged uniform and tries to tie a tourniquet around LIONEL's hand, increasingly angry, losing composure, near sobs—)

ELTON (cont.)

We just gotta get back to our Macon. We got to get out of this hellhole, Lionel. We just gotta get out. When we gonna get back to Macon? Why we holed up here, Lionel? You tell me? You go and tell me!

LIONEL

> (Remains in daze throughout rest of scene)

What'd he mean "none of my bee's wax"?

ELTON

    (Panic)

They're killin' us in here, these bluebellies!

LIONEL

What'd he mean, "none of my bee's wax"?

    (SOUND: Same Stephen Foster MUSIC starts to swell.)

LIONEL (cont.)

There's the music again, Eltie. Do ya' hear the music?

ELTON

    (Exasperated)

I don't hear no music!

LIONEL

What he mean, "none of my bee's wax"?

ELTON

We gotta git back to Georgia.

    (HE holds LIONEL, starts to gently rock HIM back and
    forth, as though rocking a child.)

ELTON (cont.)

We gotta git back to Georgia.

    (A third soldier appears, CALEB SMITH, wearing rags,
    wearied, insipid stare. HE moves slowly, halting every ur-
    gency. HE is MUTE.)

ELTON (cont.)

Caleb, you help us here.

    (CALEB only moves closer and maintains HIS stare.)

ELTON (cont.)

Don't you just stand there starin', sayin' nothin', terrorizing us with
no words 'bout nothin'!

ELTON (cont.)

    (Agitated, looking up at watchtower, clutching LIONEL tighter)

Preston! You get your bluebellies down here!

    (ELTON continues to rock LIONEL.)

ELTON (cont.)

    (To CALEB)

You ever open your mouth again, it gotta be to tell us if we ever gonna get back to Macon.

    (CALEB gently shakes HIS head, "no." LIONEL continues HIS trance, ELTON is startled by CALEB's response.)

ELTON (cont.)

That mean you'll never open your mouth again or we never gonna make it back to Macon?

    (CALEB still shakes HIS head.)

ELTON (cont.)

Or does it mean you don't know nothin'?

    (CALEB still shaking HIS head.)

    (ELTON continues to rock LIONEL.)

LIONEL

    (Softly)

What'd he mean "none of my bees-wax"?

    (CALEB slowly walks closer, until HE is next to THEM, bends over and looks THEM both in the face.)

    (ELTON, disgusted, pulls HIS face back.)

ELTON

What?!

    (CALEB bends to look LIONEL in the eyes. THEY are an inch apart.)

LIONEL

What'd they mean "none of my beeswax"?

> (CALEB only stares into HIS eyes.)

LIONEL (cont.)

> (Pleads)

What'd they mean "none of my beeswax"?

> (CALEB bends to one knee, continues to stare, then kisses
> LIONEL on the cheek, rises, puts HIS hands on each man's
> shoulder and slowly walks away—watched closely, suspi-
> ciously by ELTON.)

> (LIONEL rises, starts to follow CALEB.)

ELTON

Lionel, I ain't goin' where he's goin'.

> (ELTON follows, wandering off.)

> (NOTE REGARDING SCENE CHANGES:

> All scene changes should be done WITHOUT a BLACK-
> OUT, ELTON and LIONEL may exit amid the flurry of
> activity to set up the Edie McDonald show. THEY share
> the same space, oblivious to the next scene—two separate
> worlds criss-crossing without recognition.)

Scene Two

SETTING: The "Edie McDonald Show," a 1990's-styled television talk show, is in production. EDIE hosts her show from the aisles of the theater, AUDIENCE PARTIC-IPANTS are strewn throughout the theater. EDIE holds court with MICROPHONE in hand, speaking directly to the GUESTS and fielding questions from AUDIENCE PARTICIPANTS.

    It is important to understand that EDIE takes herself very seriously, and should adeptly transcend any "caricatured" sensibility. . . .

    The TWO GUESTS are seated on the platform that has just been constructed in the previous scene. A floor DIRECTOR/PRODUCER, wearing head-phones, carrying a clipboard, lifting "LAUGH" and "APPLAUSE" signs oversees the production. HOUSE LIGHTS ARE ON.

AT RISE: SOUND: APPLAUSE TRACK is playing over SHOW THEME (any arcane, carnival ditty). The DIRECTOR/PRODUCER holds up "APPLAUSE" sign, AUDIENCE "PLANTS" obey, hopefully fol-lowed by AUDIENCE.

    (EDIE glides down center aisle, turns to AUDIENCE—)

EDIE
And welcome back to the "Edie McDonald Show," and I'm—

AUDIENCE PLANTS

Edie McDonald!

> (SOUND: Two-second LAUGH TRACK)

EDIE

Don't forget that tomorrow on our show we'll be talking to women who refuse to French kiss their husbands. In case you've just joined us, today we're talking to people who wish they were animals. No, not to be mistaken for those who want to be in a Frat Boy movie—wear togas, chug beer, grope women and act like animals—no, we're talking people who actually want to be monkeys, lions and tigers and bears, oh boy . . . and—well, let's find out from them. Anna Johnson from Wapakoneta, Ohio—

> (SOUND: Short APPLAUSE TRACK)

EDIE (cont.)

Welcome to the "Edie McDonald Show" and I'm—

AUDIENCE PLANTS

Edie McDonald!

> (SOUND: Two-second LAUGH TRACK)

EDIE

Anna, tell us about your strong desire to be an animal.

ANNA

I'm, I'm, ah, I'm sick of humanity.

EDIE

So you're sick of humanity.

> (EDIE turns subtly to AUDIENCE, slight roll of the eye—
> this is going to be a tough one. EDIE with a bolt of new
> energy, presses ever onward. . . .)

EDIE (cont.)

Of course, we can understand; we've all been to the place where

EDIE (cont.)

we've been hurt, where people have let us down, pushed us aside—
treated us like animals.

ANNA

I was treated like an animal, an abusive mother and an incompetent father . . . it's a story you've heard a million times. It's all the
same.

EDIE

(Protesting)

No, Anna— it's not something we've heard a million times. It's
not all the same. Each individual has their own story, their own
burden, their own path, their own—

ANNA

(Interrupts)

Can I tell you what animal I want to be?

EDIE

We'd prefer getting to know you first.

ANNA

Incompetent mother, abusive father.

EDIE

Anna, so, obviously you're talking about a very painful childhood.

ANNA

Yes.

EDIE

Incompetent father, abusive mother?

ANNA

Yes.

EDIE

. . . Could we start with your incompetent father?

ANNA

Absent. Lifeless. His only commitment was to the Browns.

EDIE

The Browns?

ANNA

He loves the Cleveland Browns and I understand he's been equally committed to at least two hours of online videos every day the last couple of years. I think I hate him. I know I hate him. I've hated him for a long time.

EDIE

. . . And you're not sending any Father's Day cards any time soon.

ANNA

Incompetent father, abusive mother . . . and you have heard it a million times.

EDIE

You're obviously a very bitter woman.

ANNA

Can I tell you what animal I want to be?

EDIE

What about your abusive mother?

ANNA

Don't tell me you have her backstage ready to make a surprise appearance.

EDIE

No.

ANNA
Good. I think I hate her. I know I hate her. In fact, I know I've hated her for a long time. Can I tell you what animal I want to be?

EDIE
(Pause, unsure of how to turn. SHE gives in.)
Okay, okay, what animal would you like to be?

ANNA
(Quietly)
A muskrat.

EDIE
A what? I'm sorry, Anna, we couldn't hear you.

ANNA
(Louder)
A muskrat.

EDIE
I'm sorry, but this is national television, you're gonna have to shout so the viewers in Montana can hear you.
(SOUND: Two-second LAUGH TRACK)

ANNA
(SCREAMS)
A muskrat! I wanna be a muskrat!!

EDIE
But wait a minute, Anna. You indicated to my producers that you wanted to be a cat, but not a declawed cat. In fact, the word "declawed" in capital letters. See here.
(SHE shows ANNA the word)
So what made you change from wanting to be a cat to a muskrat?
(ANNA even more frightened.)

EDIE (cont.)

Can you tell us, Anna?

ANNA

    (Venomously spewing HER confession)

I don't want to be a cat anymore because cats sit in the laps of people!! I think I hate people. I know I hate people. In fact, I've hated people for a long time!

    (ANNA is drained.)

EDIE

    (Sincerely)

Don't worry, Anna— no one's going to make you sit on their lap.

    (AUDIENCE responds.)

    (SOUND: Two second LAUGH TRACK)

EDIE (cont.)

Okay, let's meet our second guest. He's from Marshall, Michigan; his name is Steve Morgan and he wants to be a—

    (SHE looks at card)

a sea turtle, and I hope you haven't changed your mind.

    (SOUND: Two second LAUGH TRACK)

STEVE

No, Edie, I haven't and never will.

EDIE

But, Steve, a cat perhaps; maybe even a muskrat, but a sea turtle?

    (SOUND: Two second LAUGH TRACK)

STEVE

Edie, to tell the truth, this desire to become a sea turtle all started when I realized I was tired of being conscious of my own existence, of being overtaken by the angst of non-being, of being faced with the terror of commitment—

(EDIE jumps on STAGE, one arm outstretched, as though holding a stop sign.)

EDIE

(LAUGHS slightly)

Okay, now that's something a lot of us have heard before—"terror of commitment." So, ah, animals make no commitments?

STEVE

Not unless you're a Canadian goose or a lap dog.

ANNA

(Trance-like)

I've heard that before.

EDIE

I'm sorry, Anna—what did you say?

ANNA

(On the edge emotionally, SHE turns to STEVE)

Terror of commitment?!

STEVE

(Inches away from HER, nervous)

Y-yes.

ANNA

(Getting in STEVE's face)

Terror of commitment?!!

(ANNA snaps, leaps out of HER chair and attacks STEVE with a deafening SCREAM—)

ANNA

I'll give you terror of commitment!!

(ANNA is choking STEVE, who is terrorized by the outburst.)

EDIE

Security!

> (The DIRECTOR/PRODUCER jumps on the platform and attempts to separate ANNA from STEVE. STEVE tries to escape, ANNA jumps on HIS back, pounding away. The DIRECTOR/PRODUCER finally succeeds in separating THEM, only after STEVE has stumbled to the STAGE floor, where in panic, HE starts moving HIS arms and legs, swimming away like a TURTLE.)
>
> (ANNA is pulled OFFSTAGE as SHE continues to SCREAM—)

ANNA

I'll show you terror of commitment!!

> (STEVE is coughing, trying to shake off the attack, continuing to swim. EDIE, thrilled by the outburst, thrusts HER microphone in STEVE's face—)

STEVE

See why I want to be a sea turtle?

EDIE

> (to AUDIENCE/CAMERA)

When we come back we'll see if we can settle Anna down and get to the bottom of her pain with a psychologist who can warn us of the hidden dangers lurking in the animal kingdom.

DIRECTOR/PRODUCER

> (To CREW)

All right, let's try to tie this thing down!

> (To EDIE)

We're not talking about a regular break here, are we Edie?

EDIE

Why not?

DIRECTOR/PRODUCER

Okay, I double dare ya'—

> (ANNA comes SCREAMING through the studio, chasing STEVE.)

DIRECTOR/PRODUCER (cont.)

To get the muskrat back in the cage!

EDIE

Okay, you're right. Let's take five.

DIRECTOR/PRODUCER

Ah, by the way, do you think this is the kind of thing the syndicators are trying to stop?

EDIE

Why, you didn't think that segment was educational?

> (To AUDIENCE, a bit perturbed)

Didn't you think that segment was informative?

AUDIENCE MEMBER

> (Gushing)

We love you, Edie!

EDIE

Thank you. That means a lot to me. Maybe you'll never know how much.

> (Readdressing whole AUDIENCE)

Weren't there educational elements in that segment?

AUDIENCE MEMBERS

Yes!

EDIE

I think it can be easily argued that there is value in finding social

EDIE (cont.)

specimens that force us to reflect on our culture at large and the conditions that have created these personal crises. Am I right?

AUDIENCE MEMBERS

Yes!

EDIE

I mean I'm getting pressure from syndicators to turn this kind of thing down. I mean, what kind of thing? I'm not talking about close-ups on napping nudists who vote Republican! I'm talking about honestly disturbed individuals in crisis here! Honestly disturbed individuals who need love.

AUDIENCE MEMBER

We love you, Edie!

(EDIE stops, slightly irritated, turns to this admirer—)

EDIE

Didn't you just say that?

AUDIENCE MEMBER

Yes, but I do love you— I can't help it!

EDIE

Thank you, thank you for loving me.

DIRECTOR/PRODUCER

(to CAMERA OPERATOR)

Let's get this.

(EDIE's diatribe is caught by camera. . . .)

EDIE

(Turning to whole AUDIENCE, angry)

And would the syndicators really feel better about this show if I rolled a late night talk show-style desk, hired a big band and

EDIE (cont.)

asked the movie "stars" about how to gaze upon them with greater wonder? How to touch the hem of their garment? Line up for communion with the gods! Mt. Olympus from the convenience of the remote control!

(Another gear, mocking mad as though interviewing a Hollywood personality)

Oh, do please tell us 'bout your next project! Your opinions on Central Park Pet police! How 'bout the rain forests? Are you or are you not for world peace? Is that really more culturally relevant? Don't anyone tell me that's more of a public service!

AUDIENCE MEMBER

(Same as before)

We love you, Edie!

EDIE

Thank you. We all need to be loved.

(EDIE walks off. . . .)

Scene Three

SETTING: The prison yard is empty, August, 1864.

AT RISE: Only the SOUND of orchestrated Stephen Foster.
            LIGHTS OFF of platform.

> (LIONEL enters in silence. HE is more haggard, sickly, HIS
> hand bandaged and missing its forefinger. HE just stares at
> the fence and the platform on the other side.)
>
> (ELTON enters with HARMONICA, offering it to LIONEL.
> ELTON also looks more worn, ragged. THEY are swatting
> MOSQUITOES throughout scene.)

ELTON
You gonna play this, or what ol' man?

> (LIONEL breaks out into a grin. HE pulls a handful of dirt
> from HIS pocket and shows it to ELTON. HE also shows
> ELTON a STONE)

LIONEL
Lookie here, Eltie.

> (Holding stone aloft)

Ain't somethin' peculiar about that rock?

> (ELTON looks up at it, still in LIONEL's hand. Pause.)

ELTON
Looks just like a rock to me.

LIONEL
You sure you don't see nothin' peculiar?

ELTON

No, sure don't.

LIONEL

Well, then maybe I need to move it around a bit so you can see it just right.

>(LIONEL, still holding the palm-sized stone in HIS hand, begins moving it slightly, changing the angle for ELTON. ELTON remains unimpressed.)

ELTON

It don't make no difference. Still looks like a plain old rock to me.

LIONEL

>(Protesting)

Noo.

>(Brings the stone closer to HIS face and adjusts the angle and shows it to ELTON)

You mean to tell me that don't look like no state of Georgia to you?

>(Puts it closer in ELTON's face)

Lookie there,

>(Fingers the side of the stone)

There's the Atlantic coast.

>(Points on stone with finger)

There's Savannah, Atlanta . . . and there's Macon.

ELTON

Well, I can kinda see it, sort of.

LIONEL

Found it last night diggin'.

ELTON

You stay down there long enough, and everything start to look like where you'd rather be, don't it?

>   (LIONEL suddenly turns to face ELTON, arrested by the thought, and discouragedly drops the stone.)

ELTON (cont.)

But it did kinda look like Georgia.

LIONEL

No, it didn't. It didn't, did it?

ELTON

I thought it did. Really.

LIONEL

Eltie, we're gonna get ourselves back to Macon.

>   (HE puts dirt back in pocket.)

ELTON

>   (LAUGHS)

How far you get last night?

LIONEL

A good eighteen inches.

ELTON

Only eighteen inches? Well, then we ain't gettin' back to Macon before any time soon. What do you mean eighteen inches? Frederick and I got almost four feet the other night. You sleepin' on the job or what?

LIONEL

Lotta rocks, Eltie; lotta rocks. I figured we's right about . . .

>   (HE walks six-seven feet farther away from the fence and

marks the spot with a little jump, the most emphasis HE
can muster)

LIONEL (cont.)
here.

ELTON
Don't jump like that or you gonna 'cause a cave-in!

LIONEL
(LAUGHS)
No feeble legs gonna 'cause no cave-in.
(HE lowers HIS voice)
I am worried about under that fence though. No tellin' how deep it
goes. So we might need to dig a bit deeper to get under it.
(HE LAUGHS)
I'll just make sure it's done on your night!

ELTON
(Looking up at guard tower, lowers voice)
Don't say nothin' more, Preston's boys lookin' this way.
(LIONEL joins in looking. Smiles. Waves.)

LIONEL
Well, I'll just wave then and practice pointin' things out with my
three fingered hand, so I'll be good and sharp when it opens—

ELTON
Lionel Stubbs, ever the tour guide.
(LIONEL lifts bandaged hand and points OFFSTAGE.)

LIONEL
And over here's the mess hall where they make us monkeys line
up, lettin' us be pushin' and shovin' and fightin' 'mongst outselves
knowin' there ain't enough food to feed half of us. And the hungry

LIONEL (cont.)

Rebs just let somebody fall over, knowin' that's one less mouth they gotta compete with.

ELTON

Save your breath for the crowds; they the ones need to hear 'em, not Preston and his Fed boys.

> (STAGEHAND walks onto platform as LIGHTS rise. HE nails a wooden sign to DOWNSTAGE side of platform that reads: "ADMISSION 15 CENTS, REFRESHMENTS SERVED BELOW.")
>
> (LIONEL and ELTON stare in silence, disbelievingly.)

LIONEL

They're openin' a trifle early today.

ELTON

Early bird gets the worm.

LIONEL

You mean the fifteen cents and the nickel lemon pop.

> (The planted AUDIENCE MEMBERS, now having thrown on 19th century garb, walk onto platform in the back of the theatre. Some carry binoculars, others drinks, popcorn, and cakes. THEY gape at the prisoners and respond to their every movement.)

ELTON

Goofy lookin' folk, don't ya' think, Lionel?

> (LIONEL raises HIS bandaged hand and restarts HIS diatribe.)

LIONEL

And over there, ladies and gentlemen, in those cozy barracks most people call tents, three men died of exposure since we last saw you yesterday—

(ONLOOKERS not listening.)

ONE ONLOOKER
(SHOUTS)
Hey, you Johnny Rebs! We didn't pay no fifteen pennies to see you just stand around. We want our money's worth!

(To the others)
How 'bout it folks?!

(The OTHERS chime in.)

ELTON
They don't wanna hear your sermons. I think they like our animal act the best.

(ELTON begins to prance around like a MONKEY. The ONLOOKERS love it, some start to APPLAUD.)

ELTON (cont.)
Lookie here, Lionel, them Yankees love it!

LIONEL
Sure do.

ELTON
Maybe we can get 'em to throw us some peanuts.

LIONEL
Or maybe if we roared like lions they throw us some meat.

ELTON
No, Lionel, let's be monkeys today!

(ELTON moves monkey-like into LIONEL's face and pronounces mockingly—)
I've never been a cur-ee-os-city before.

(ELTON lets off HIS monkey SQUEEL.)

(LIONEL stares at the observation tower through the rest of the scene.)

LIONEL

Man who built that tower of Babel makin' a fortune, while we rot. He's a bastard.

(CALEB enters, shaking HIS head aggressively, behind LIONEL and ELTON, drinking in the scene, giving HIS silent commentary. LIONEL and ELTON do not see CALEB.)

ELTON

(Continuing HIS monkey antics)

I heard the new one's makin' even more money. Good, more peanuts for us monkeys! What d'ya know, fifteen cents to see our entertainin' Southern selves.

LIONEL

With all this competition, wonder how long 'fore the price for admission drops to a measly dime.

ELTON

Oh, the wonders of free enterprise.

LIONEL

You'd think they'd have more to do than look at our ugly selves.

ELTON

You speak for youssel, old man.

(ELTON LAUGHS. LIONEL doesn't, HE just keeps staring. The ONLOOKERS are enjoying themselves. A few pieces of POPCORN are hurled over the fence. ELTON pounces on THEM.)

LIONEL

(Looking at ONLOOKERS)

These Yankees are the real patriots— it pronounced P-A-Y triots up here in handy-dandy Elmira.

(Shakes HIS head)

Eltie, I miss my family.

(CALEB still shaking HIS head.)

ELTON

(Scratching under arm)

Me, too.

LIONEL

Wonder what they'd pay to see us make out like monkeys.

(LIONEL begins to scratch under HIS arm, slowly crouch over in monkey pose.)

(CALEB picks up STONE dropped by LIONEL, holds it aloft, studies it, still unseen . . . puts it in HIS pocket. Walks off, shaking head.)

LIONEL (cont.)

Gonna get three feet tomorrow night. Maybe more.

ELTON

(Smiles)

Probably less.

LIONEL

(Deadpanned)

Maybe I can find more rocks the shape of Georgia.

(ELTON looks at LIONEL, maintains smile.)

(THEY wander off, scratching underarms.)

Scene Four

SETTING: "The Edie McDonald" set.

AT RISE: EDIE is hovered over STEVE, attempting to help HIM recover from ANNA's attack.

DIRECTOR/PRODUCER
We about ready to roll, Edie?

EDIE
Give us another minute. Somebody go find our muskrat friend.

    (BILL McDONALD, Edie's husband, walks toward the platform.)

BILL
You're not going to catch her; she ran screaming out the side door.

EDIE
    (Still attending to STEVE)
We've only taped one segment, honey. How about meeting me for lunch?

BILL
No. I have something to tell you and I want the cameras on.

EDIE
Bill, we can talk about it at lunch— can't it wait that long, darling?

BILL
You're going to love it. I'm sure it's something you can use.

EDIE

Bill, honey, don't push it.

BILL

I want it taped; besides, it's going to take a while to find your guest.

>	(BILL takes Edie's vacated seat.)

EDIE

Bill, can't we talk about it some other time?

>	(BILL sits in chair.)

BILL

No.

EDIE

>	(To DIRECTOR/PRODUCER, throwing up arms, unsure of what to do)

Help me here.

DIRECTOR/PRODUCER

It's your show, Edie.

EDIE

Okay, let's roll!

>	(DIRECTOR/PRODUCER points to EDIE, returning from break.)
>	(SOUND: TAPED APPLAUSE.)

EDIE (cont.)

We're back, but Anna has run away. So, my husband— you all know my lover man, Billy-boy McDonald, an animal in his own way—

>	(The AUDIENCE SQUEELS with glee.)
>	(SOUND: two seconds of TAPED APPLAUSE)

EDIE (cont.)

So my Billy has something he wanted to say to me on camera. It better be romantic. What's so special that you just have to share it with my audience?

BILL

(Pauses)

I'm leaving you.

EDIE

What?!

BILL

It's over. I'm doing it for you, dear. None of your rivals can touch this television moment. I'm only thinking of you, dear.

EDIE

What are you saying?

DIRECTOR/PRODUCER

Edie, let's stop the tape!

EDIE

(Trying to control herself)

No, uh— of course not, keep rolling.

DIRECTOR/PRODUCER

Edie, I really think—

EDIE

(Forcefully)

Keep rolling!

(SHE sizes up BILL, still stunned, lining HIM up in HER crosshairs . . . making the most of the moment—a deep cleansing sigh. . . .)

EDIE (cont.)

Billy . . . darling, did I read my card right? You're leaving me?

BILL

I thought you could use a little publicity.

EDIE

>   (Still encircling, unsure. . . .)

How sweet, Billy— but you've never been anything but sweet. . . .
You're leaving me?

BILL

Just think of the increased amount of empathy for you—captain of
the broken hearts.

EDIE

You're taking it for granted that you've broken my heart.

BILL

Okay, so maybe I haven't broken your heart. That possibility some-
how fits, too.

EDIE

All things are possible, including leaving this show.

BILL

Oh, sure, now you're breaking the nation's heart.

EDIE

It might be the most relevant thing I've ever done.

BILL

Yes, you were always good at leaving relevance to everyone else.

EDIE

You're a real riot, Billy-dear.

(BILL is starting to get slightly uncomfortable. SHE looks
blankly at HIM.)

BILL

That's all I wanted to say, Edie-dear.

DIRECTOR/PRODUCER

Edie—

EDIE

Shut-up, Mick; we're not finished here, Billy-darling isn't finished
with his clever attempt to humiliate me. Have you, Billy, darling?

BILL

I'm only thinking of you, dear. I've been a guest on your show
long enough.

EDIE

Oh, Bill, you're outdoing yourself. Did you just think of that clever
line right on the spot? Or is it a sixteenth draft? I'll bet you've been
practicing it for a while now.

(Quoting HIM, mocking)

I've been a guest on your show long enough.

BILL

Go to hell, Edie.

EDIE

That's quite a directive for an agnostic, Bill-dearie. Oh,
Bill—I'm suddenly,

(Feigning shock)

overwhelmed by your sense of poetic justice. . . .

(Snapping out of it, SHE starts pacing in quick, jerky
movements)

BILL

That's about all I needed—

EDIE

Are you—

> (Slowly, satirically)

turning the channel, Billy-pooh?—

BILL

. . . to say.

EDIE

What is it, another talk-show host with bigger boobs, better hair?

BILL

Shut-up, Edie.

EDIE

Why? You're successfully created a sizzling segment here. My heart's breaking, Billy-dear, and I'm

> (Turns to camera, SHOUTS)

ASKING the camera to get a close-up of my shocked face! . . .

> (Without missing a beat is recomposed)

while you sit there, Billy-love, so I can

> (a beat)

just look at you and adore you one last time.

> (BILL starts to get up; SHE embraces HIM, gives HIM one long KISS. HE is non-responsive. . . .)

BILL

That's about all, Edie.

EDIE

Oh, but Billy-dearest, you chose the arena and the scene's not over until America knows how puny you really are.

(BILL exits.)

EDIE (cont.)

About as sexually satisfying as a gummy bear.

> (SHE SHOUTS at HIM, very controlled, arms extended out to HER side, self-crucifying position)

It's your turn, Billy-love! Expose me! Expose me!!

> (SHE turns calmly, quietly to DIRECTOR/PRODUCER)

Okay, cut.

> (SHE looks out into the audience, wounded.)
>
> (The LIGHT on HER slowly fade.)

AUDIENCE MEMBER

> (Same as before)

We love you, Edie!

> (EDIE turns HER face to find the AUDIENCE MEMBER, and just stares at HER, insipidly . . . after several beats—)

EDIE

Thank you. We all need to be loved.

> (In a daze, SHE slowly exits.)

Scene Five

SETTING: The Elmira Prison yard, November 1864.

AT RISE: SOUND: The same Stephen Foster
ORCHESTRATION.

> (LIONEL and ELTON enter the yard with THEIR arms
> wrapped around themselves, trying to keep warm. THEIR
> clothing is more worn, ragged—pathetically inadequate for
> the Novembers of up-state New York. THEIR conversation is
> regularly interrupted by a cough that possesses THEM both.)

LIONEL
I'm hearin' the music again, Eltie. You hearin' the music?

ELTON
I'm sorry, but I ain't hearin' no music.

> (SOUND: the MUSIC continues through the scene.)

LIONEL
It's lovely.

ELTON
Believe me, ol' man, I'd like to be hearin' somethin' besides these
Yankee winds.

> (SHOUTS)

Get me to Georgia!

> (CALEB enters. Same as before, shaking HIS head.)

ELTON (cont.)

See, Caleb here ain't hearin' no music either. Course he might not be hearin' anything in that there lost head of his.

(CALEB continues to shake HIS head.)

ELTON (cont.)

Then again, he might be runnin' his mouth to Preston 'bout every knick and cranny, never know, do ya' Caleb?

(CALEB still shaking HIS head.)

ELTON (cont.)

(Starting to run with this thought)

Could be laughing at us with Preston, jabberin' away 'bout this and that.

LIONEL

He ain't laughin' at us.

ELTON

Pocketin' every little nugget, storin' up gold from the bluebellies.

LIONEL

Ain't doin' no such thing. He just shakin' his head at everything like some kindly no-nothin'. I like 'im, always have.

ELTON

Jesus liked Judas, always did.

LIONEL

So, what you sayin'?

ELTON

Among other things, don't let 'im kiss ya' agin'.

LIONEL
    (Protests)
Aww, Eltie, he ain't no Judas and I ain't no Jesus.

ELTON
Somebody tellin' Preston lots of things. I think he's just actin' the idiot. Ain't ya', Caleb?

LIONEL
Maybe he's wiser than all of us, ya' ever think a that?

ELTON
You wiser than the rest of us, aye, Caleb? You wise enough to kiss the Yankee bee-hinds?

LIONEL
Why don't ya' ask 'im some real questions?

ELTON
Like what?

LIONEL
Like what's it take for a man to be what he's supposed to be? How 'bout that one?
    (CALEB shaking head.)

ELTON
That what eatin' at your craw while you freezin' in Elmira?

LIONEL
I thought you was gonna ask him.

ELTON
He only gonna keep shakin' his head, 'til maybe it gets unshook in Preston's magnificent presence.

LIONEL

And it's what's eatin' my craw. The Lord Almighty, He knows we're here— does that mean we're supposed to be, Eltie? Can you tell me that?

ELTON

You're older than me, you should know.

LIONEL

Yeh, but you've been to church long since I have.

ELTON

What makes you think the preacher gonna talk 'bout such things in church?

LIONEL

We here 'cause we on the wrong side of this slavery thing?

ELTON

We got prisoners, too, I reckon.

LIONEL

Yeh.

    (Pause)

So, what's it take for a man to be what he's supposed to be?

ELTON

Don't take that much to be a dirt farmer, there, Lionel.

LIONEL

I reckon.

ELTON

That's how I see it. Don't take much.

LIONEL

I was jus' rememberin' that couple a weeks ago ya' figured out one of us would die 'fore Christmas.

ELTON

That's what I figured, and, sorry to say, ain't nothin' happened since helped me change my mind.

>   (LIONEL turns to CALEB.)

LIONEL

That include Caleb?

ELTON

No, hadn't figured him in on the figurin'.

>   (CALEB is shaking head.)

LIONEL

Look at 'im shakin' that head a his. Easy for me to think he knows everything. Don't ya', Caleb?

>   (CALEB continues shaking HIS head.)

LIONEL (cont.)

Well, it sounds better than another one up here.

ELTON

Another what up here and what's "it"?

LIONEL

Death and Christmas. Damn if I'll see another one here.

>   (Devilish smile)

But we ain't gonna, are we?

>   (LIONEL crouches low, ELTON follows, THEIR inter-
>   change more secretive. CALEB remains in place.)

LIONEL (cont.)

It's over sixty feet, I'm tellin' ya'.

ELTON

Not so loud. Who wants Caleb runnin' to his uncle Preston? How far from the fence?

LIONEL

He ain't gonna do nothin' but settle in. We oughta feel good about him feelin' comfortable over here.

ELTON

I'm feelin' might good. How far we from the fence?

LIONEL

I figure 'bout twenty feet. Far 'nough to not wake up Preston's Fed boys from their midnight nap.

ELTON

    (Quiet LAUGH)

Then it's on to the Pennsylvania state line, and a long, cold walk to Georgia.

LIONEL

Better than waitin' our time to die in this Yankee hell hole.

ELTON

So, it's tonight, three days 'fore that Lincoln holiday, Thanksgivin'. Happy Thanksgivin', Lionel. We're in Lincoln land, we might as well exchange the greetin's.

LIONEL

I'm thankful for one thing right now, a gift from heaven.

ELTON

What's that? That tonight's the night?

LIONEL

That and a gift right from the devil's hand.

ELTON

I thought you said it was from heaven.

LIONEL

Don't matter to me whose hand it's from—

>   (HE reaches HIS hand under HIS shirt to something
>   stashed in the beltline of HIS trousers)

only that I got my hand on it.

>   (HE lets out a giant GUFFAW)

ELTON

What you got your frost bit hand on, ol' man?

LIONEL

Look out the corner of your eye and see if there any Fed boys lookin'.

ELTON

Caleb's lookin'.

LIONEL

Caleb's at everything and still shakin' his head. Stop worryin' 'bout 'im, I tell ya'. Are the fed boys lookin'?

ELTON

>   (Looking up)

They must be lookin' at some a-ris-toe-crats over yonder and not us common folk privates.

LIONEL

Just in case move your Rebel butt in front of them boys and look over here what I got covered in my hands.

>   (ELTON complies. LIONEL quickly displays a sizeable PISTOL.)

(ELTON SHOUTS with delight.)

(CALEB still shaking, eyes unfocused, not seeing a thing.)

ELTON

Ooooeee!!!

> (LIONEL, who has remained in a crouching position, quickly drops the pistol to the ground and lies on it, face down.)

LIONEL

> (Scolds, controlled whisper)

That was loud enough to let Abe Lincoln in on our little secret! Are the Fed boys lookin'?

ELTON

> (Still excited, controlled whisper)

Ha! Still lookin' at the a-ris-toe-crats.

LIONEL

Good, I didn't want to pretend that this worn out body was doin' push-ups.

ELTON

How'd you get it?

LIONEL

One harmonica, plus all the meanin'ful trinkets I made while at my time of rest here at lovely Elmira Federal Prison.

ELTON

You always could talk the hump off a hog.

LIONEL

The ol' boy kinda saw it as a goin' away present. Now, I'm goin' to put this angel back, and you tell me if anybody's lookin'.

> (ELTON looks out of the corner of his eyes.)

ELTON

They're not lookin'.

> (LIONEL slowly moves to put the pistol back.)

ELTON (cont.)

Not lookin' . . . not lookin' . . . not lookin'.

> (LIONEL has put back the pistol.)

ELTON (cont.)

Not lookin' . . . Lookin'.

LIONEL

Wave to 'em, Eltie.

> (HE does. THEY both do.)

ELTON

> (Big smile, to LIONEL)

This is our good-bye wave, Fed boys! Too bad we can't give our final waves to the spectators in the towers.

LIONEL

Too cold for 'em to show up. 'Sides, they're probably home gettin' the Abe-Lincoln-ordered Thanksgivin' dinner ready.

ELTON

Wonder if they'd invite us?

> (THEY LAUGH.)

LIONEL

Tonight's the night.

ELTON

Know what, Lionel?

LIONEL

What?

ELTON

I'm excited, little nervous, but mostly excited.

LIONEL

Through the tunnel.

ELTON

Under the fence.

LIONEL

And through the woods to Georgia . . . and now we find out that's where the war is. Damn Sherman to hell.

ELTON

    (Looking at the sky)

Wish it'd hurry up and get nighttime.

    (CALEB walks to ELTON, stands next to HIM, looking at the sky, shaking HIS head softly.)

    (AUDIO TRANSITION)

    (EDIE's audio announcement is played in the DARK.)

EDIE

Is your life story stranger than fiction? Then call me, Edie McDonald, at 1-900-555-EDIE, that's 1-900-555-EDIE. Do you desire to love your sibling in ways that society won't accept? Then call me, Edie McDonald, at 1-900-555-EDIE, that's 1-900-555-EDIE. The cost is $3.98 for the first minute and 78 cents each additional minute.

Scene Six

SETTING: "The Edie McDonald Show" is in the midst of a taping.

AT RISE: SOUND: APPLAUSE TRACK is playing over SHOW THEME. DIRECTOR/PRODUCER holds up "AP-PLAUSE" sign, AUDIENCE "PLANTS" obey.

EDIE
And welcome back to "The Edie McDonald Show", and I'm—

AUDIENCE PLANTS
Edie McDonald!

(SOUND: Two second LAUGH TRACK)

EDIE
Today we have a very special show, a show that I think will warm your hearts. An uplifting story of two people defying all odds to beat the blight of crime and decay in their neighborhood. Two people who have sacrificed a lifetime to serve others, enhancing their community. . . .

(**LIONEL and ELTON pop up from under the PLAT-FORM to inadvertently crash the show.** THEY have just escaped the prison through THEIR tunnel, and are disoriented, but pushed by the adrenaline rush. BOTH sides are stunned by the proceedings.)

EDIE (cont.)
(Angry)
Okay, stop the tape!

EDIE (cont.)

> (To DIRECTOR/PRODUCER)

When am I going to get a director who knows how to fire idiot grips?

DIRECTOR/PRODUCER

Hey, you two ass-holes, get off the set!

EDIE

And whoever you are, you're fired!

> (LIONEL is in shock, hardly moves throughout what follows. . . .)

ELTON

> (Stunned)

Where in hell are we?

EDIE

You're wrecking a taping of the Edie McDonald Show and stop acting like an ignorant moron, and get off the damn stage before we call security!

ELTON

Wh-who are y-you?

EDIE

I'm Edie McDonald or have you been asleep for the last two years?

ELTON

Lionel, I can t-tell she's a Yankee, but she's wearin' pants and she ain't ridin' a horse. Are y-you the people waitin' in line for that observation tower?

> (DIRECTOR/PRODUCER starts to move toward the platform—)

ELTON (cont.)

> (To DIRECTOR/PRODUCER, puts up HIS fists)

No, sirree, you don't wanna be movin' any closer or—

(DIRECTOR/PRODUCER stops.)

EDIE

Okay, I'm going to give you clowns until the count of five to get off the set, and then we're calling security and your five minutes of untaped attention is going to be over. One . . .

ELTON

D-don't be threatenin' us, mam. We're on our way to Georgia to rejoin the fight and nobody gonna get in our way! We spent too—

EDIE

Two . . .

ELTON

long in that hell-hole Elmira prison, didn't we Lionel?! We didn't escape to get stopped by no britches wearin' sow who thinks she owns the world!

EDIE

Three . . .

ELTON

Lionel, tell her . . . do somethin'! We're movin' through here, lady, and you can go call Preston, but we'll be long gone!

EDIE

Four . . .

>   (ELTON starts to move off the platform. LIONEL re-mains frozen.)

EDIE (cont.)

Five! Security!! I want security now! Take these maniacs someplace to rot!

>   (A UNIFORMED SECURITY OFFICER approaches the platform.)

(LIONEL snaps out of it, pulls out HIS PISTOL. SECURITY OFFICER freezes.)

LIONEL

Now I don't know who you are, and I don't know where I am, but Eltie and me is headed for Georgia to kill some more Yankees, and I won't mind killin' some on the way.

EDIE

(To HER DIRECTOR/PRODUCER, bright idea)

Mick, roll the tape!

(DIRECTOR/PRODUCER quietly speaks through headset, ordering the scene recorded.)

LIONEL

(Interrogating, jumpy)

What's "roll the tape" mean?

EDIE

(Trying to sooth, SHE is frightened, but confident SHE hasn't met a troubled soul SHE couldn't undress)

Well, as host of this show, I think it would be a good idea to let the rest of the country participate in this very . . .

(Searching for word)

intriguing change of events.

ELTON

Lionel, let's get outta here!

LIONEL

What d'ya' mean the "rest of the country"?!

EDIE

Sir, "The Edie McDonald Show" is on in hundreds of markets in all fifty states.

LIONEL

Where they get fifty states?

ELTON

Lionel, c'mon. Let's get out of here!

LIONEL

What d'ya mean fifty states?! Whose got fifty states?!

EDIE

Lionel, my show is shown all over the country. New York, Seattle, Atlanta—

LIONEL

Macon?

EDIE

I'm sure we're on in Macon.

LIONEL

L-look, lady. I-I don't know what foolhardy Yankee weapon you talkin' about, but it ain't takin' over no Georgia—

ELTON

C'mon, Lionel!! I'm runnin' out a here with or without ya'!

EDIE

I think if you put down your gun, Mr. Lionel, we could talk with the country and have a wonderfully unique segment.

(Starts to walk toward LIONEL, HE takes a step back)

I'm sure those "condescending do-gooders" wouldn't mind being taped later. I mean, it's not every day that we get to talk to kindly, delusional southerners still fighting the Civil War.

LIONEL

What d'ya mean, "delusional." You tryin' to get fancy with me?

EDIE

By no means, sir. We only want you to put your gun away, sit down and try to relax.

LIONEL

    (Referring to television cameras)

I'll think about relaxin' when you turn those Yankee cannons around.

EDIE

Sir, I assure you those aren't cannons. They're television cameras. Please, tell us why you're so angry.

LIONEL

Why should I believe you?!

    (Shows HIS gun)

Stop pointin' those cannons at me!

ELTON

Lionel, let's git outta here!

EDIE

Lionel, look— instead of turning the cameras around, why don't we give one to you so you can point it at us.

ELTON

Let good enough alone, ol' man, and let's get outta here! You wanna see your family or not?

EDIE

Mick, pull the boys closer and show our guest how he can point this cannon at us.

    (A CAMERA OPERATOR brings the CAMERA to LIO-
    NEL, who starts to back away.)

EDIE (cont.)

We'll even show you how to point it right at my head if you'll only put down your gun and let me talk to you some more.

LIONEL

(Angrily)

That'll be enough, just keep 'em turned around.

EDIE

Lionel, why are you so angry? There's no reason for you to be holding that gun. Why don't you put it down so we can—

LIONEL

I ain't puttin' nothin' down.

EDIE

Tell us why you're angry. We want to understand your pain. Lionel, help us feel it with you. America wants to understand you.

ELTON

Believe me, mam, he don't need nobody understandin' him. C'mon, Lionel. Stop bein' a fool!

EDIE

No, ah, just a minute, Lionel. Tell us a little about yourself—

LIONEL

What fool wanna hear me talk 'bout myself?

EDIE

Believe me, a lot of "fools" would. Lionel, why are you so angry? What inside you has created this hatred? Can you tell us about it?

LIONEL

What gentleman you ever know liked talkin' 'bout himself? What you tryin' to do, grab my soul?

EDIE

(Lets off tension releasing sigh, thinking through next move)
Lionel, can we get you to sit down and put away your gun? No
one here is interested in hurting you, capturing you, or whatever.
So please—

ELTON

So why we stayin', Lionel? They ain't gonna stop us. Let's go!

LIONEL

'Cause I think I escaped a year of hell in Elmira to come face to face
with the devil. This devil tryin' to wage war with my soul. This may
be my destiny, to look her eye to eye and spit.

EDIE

So, Lionel . . . I'm the . . . devil?

LIONEL

I can tell you're possessed. And you're tryin' to possess my head
and you may just—

EDIE

So . . . I'm not the devil, I'm only . . . possessed.

LIONEL

(Thrusting pistol)
And you're tryin' to get in my head, steal my soul. I might of escaped to bring you a message, lady.

ELTON

I'm goin', ol' man; I'll meet you on down the road. Stop messin'
with these fools.

(LIONEL does not respond, not even a glance Elton's way.)

LIONEL

I escaped to bring you a message, lady.

ELTON
> (Moving closer to exit)

Lionel, let's go!

EDIE

And what's the message, Lionel. Please tell me the message. Tell . . . tell America the message.

LIONEL

You're possessed.

EDIE

Yes, I heard that before.

> (Contemplating next move)

Let's start over. Lionel, can we start over?

> (SHE moves closer.)

You see this is a television show called, "The Edie McDonald Show", and I'm—

ONE AUDIENCE MEMBER

Edie McDonald!!

> (The LAUGH TRACK starts to play.)

LIONEL

Who's laughin' at me? I hear people laughin' at me!

> (EDIE whirls around, commanding the BOOTH—)

EDIE

Turn that off!

> (The LAUGH TRACK is ABRUPTLY TURNED OFF.)

EDIE (cont.)

Now, ah, let me try again—

LIONEL

(Threatening with pistol)

Where'd that come from? That laughin', where those people hidin'?!

EDIE

(Slight, nervous LAUGH)

That was a mistake. I'm sorry.

(The LAUGH TRACK continues, only this time with REVERB that INCREASES as the VOLUME INCREASES through the rest of the play.)

(LIONEL sticks pistol out menacingly, angrily.)

LIONEL

Who's laughin' at me?! I hear people laughin' at me!

ELTON

Nobody laughin' at you, you ol' fool! Let's go!

(ELTON exits.)

LIONEL

I hear people laughin'! Who's laughin' at me?!

EDIE

(Approaches, trying to assure)

Believe me, Lionel, nobody's laughing at you.

LIONEL

(Panicking)

Get 'em to stop!

EDIE

Lionel, I don't hear any laughter. Nobody's laughing. Please sit down and tell us—

LIONEL

Get 'em to stop!!

ELTON

>(SHOUTING OFFSTAGE)

C'mon, Lionel!

>(EDIE continues to approach, attempts to soothe.)

EDIE

Lionel, there's no one laughing.

>(SHE's right next to LIONEL.)
>(The LAUGH TRACK gets louder.)

LIONEL

>(SCREAMS)

Stop it!!

>(LIONEL grabs EDIE and wraps one of HIS arms around HER neck. Brandishes pistol menacingly to the audience.)

LIONEL (cont.)

I said stop it!!

>(The LAUGH TRACK gets louder still.)
>(The DIRECTOR/PRODUCER tries to approach.)

DIRECTOR/PRODUCER

Hey, look, man— we don't know what laughter you're hearing. We're sorry 'bout that little glitch a minute ago, but we don't—

>(LIONEL waves the gun at the DIRECTOR/PRODUCER, who backs off.)

EDIE

>(CRYING, PLEADING—)

We don't know what—

LIONEL

I asked you to stop it!

EDIE

Please don't shoot me, mister! God have mercy, have mercy!!!

LIONEL

Nooo! You have mercy!!

EDIE

What d'ya want from me?! What d'ya want from me?!! I'll do anything you want, anything you want!!!

    (The REVERBED LAUGH TRACK is louder.)

LIONEL

    (SCREAMING at the top of HIS lungs)

Stop it!!!

    (The LAUGHTER ONLY GETS LOUDER.)

EDIE

I can't stop it! I can't stop it!! I don't know what to stop, don't know what to—

    (LAUGH TRACK is LOUDER. LIONEL, pulled in by its
    distractive mockery, does not even realize that HIS GRIP on
    EDIE has loosened. EDIE, out of HIS GRIP, crumbles to the
    floor, CRYING.)
    (The LAUGH TRACK is LOUDER.)

LIONEL

    (SCREAMING in agony.)

Make them stop it!!!

    (LAUGH TRACK DRONES ON. . . .)
    (LIONEL slowly points gun at HIS HEAD and SCREAMS—)

LIONEL (cont.)

STOOOOP!!!

> (HE FIRES A BULLET into HIS SKULL and is tossed to the floor.)
>
> (The LAUGH TRACK continues. ELTON REENTERS, running, and freezes when HE sees LIONEL. EDIE SOBS quietly.)
>
> (ELTON then lunges to embrace LIONEL.)

ELTON

I told ya' we had to get back home! I told ya' not to be messin' with these bluebellies. . . .

> (HE starts to drag LIONEL OFFSTAGE, continuing HIS lament. . . .)
>
> (DIRECTOR/PRODUCER gingerly approaches a quietly weeping EDIE.)

DIRECTOR/PRODUCER

> (Whispering)

Edie . . . Hey, Edie—

> (EDIE turns to face DIRECTOR/PRODUCER.)

DIRECTOR/PRODUCER (cont.)

I, ah, think we got everything.

> (EDIE does not respond, only a blank stare. The DIRECTOR/PRODUCER helps HER up, starts to walk HER OFFSTAGE.)

AUDIENCE MEMBER

> (Same as before)

We love you, Edie.

> (EDIE and the DIRECTOR/PRODUCER exit. After a few beats . . .)
>
> (CALEB breaks into the studio in the same manner as HIS

confederate mates. HE wears exactly the same expression as before, shaking HIS head looking at audience.)

(HE scans the faces. Pulls out LIONEL's STONE HE had pocketed earlier.)

(Lifts it above HIS face and studies carefully and then while still studying the stone, mutters with slight impediment. . . .)

CALEB

G-Georgia. . . .

(HE puts the stone back in pocket and wanders off. . . .)

(The LIGHTS finish FADING.)

END OF PLAY